D1522990

Baby Animals

A Baby Sea Otter Story

by Martha E. H. Rustad

Consulting Editor: Gail Saunders-Smith, PhD

CAPSTONE PRESS
a capstone imprint

Rock-a-bye, baby.

Ocean waves gently rock

a mother sea otter.

She holds her baby pup

on her belly.

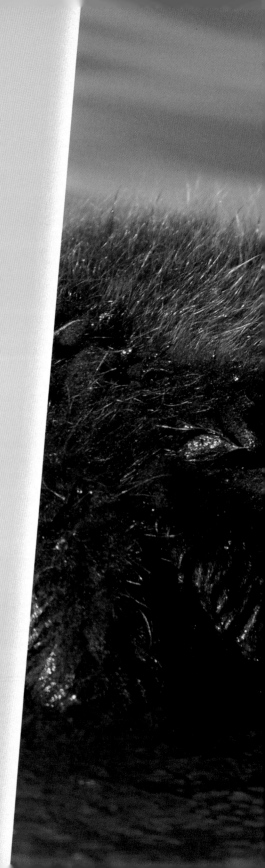

Squeal! The hungry pup
squeaks loudly. Mom feeds
her baby milk from her body.
The sleepy pup dozes
in its watery home.

With her paws, mom grooms
her baby. Poof! She blows air
into its fur. The air keeps
the pup warm and helps it float.

Time to eat! The hungry mom
wraps her pup safely in kelp.
She dives underwater
to find food.

Mom is back.

She pulls a crab out

of her armpit pocket.

Gulp! The pup hungrily eats

the food she shares.

Mom gives her pup

swimming lessons.

Paddle your back feet.

Close your ears and nose.

Now dive!

Pups learn to find food

in the kelp forest.

Use your whiskers to find prey.

Use a rock to open shells.

Tap, crack! Keep on trying.

Bath time! Pups learn to groom their thick fur. Bend and stretch to reach your back. Clean fur helps sea otters stay warm.

Tag, you're it.

You can't catch me!

Sea otter pups play together.

Bye, mom!

At six months old,

pups are on their own.

They will find a mate

in their ocean home.

Glossary

doze—to sleep lightly for a short time

groom—to clean one's fur; a female sea otter grooms her pup's fur

kelp—a type of seaweed

mate—a male or female partner of a pair of animals

prey—an animal that is hunted and eaten by another animal; sea otters eat clams, sea stars, sea urchins, crabs, and other small sea animals

whisker—a long, stiff hair near the mouth of some mammals; sea otters use their whiskers to feel

Read More

Rake, Jody Sullivan. *Sea Otters*. Under the Sea. Mankato, Minn.: Capstone Press, 2008.

Waxman, Laura Hamilton. *Let's Look at Sea Otters*. Lightning Bolt Books: Animal Close-Ups. Minneapolis: Lerner Publications Company, 2011.

Wendorff, Anne. *Sea Otters*. Blastoff! Readers: Oceans Alive. Minneapolis: Bellwether Media, 2009.

Internet Sites

FactHound offers a safe, fun way to find Internet sites related to this book. All of the sites on FactHound have been researched by our staff.

Here's all you do:

Visit *www.facthound.com*

Type in this code: 9781429660648

Check out projects, games and lots more at
www.capstonekids.com

Pebble Plus is published by Capstone Press,
151 Good Counsel Drive, P.O. Box 669, Mankato, Minnesota 56002.
www.capstonepub.com

Books published by Capstone Press are manufactured with paper
containing at least 10 percent post-consumer waste.

Library of Congress Cataloging-in-Publication Data
Rustad, Martha E. H. (Martha Elizabeth Hillman), 1975–
  A baby sea otter story / by Martha E. H. Rustad.
    p. cm.—(Pebble plus. Baby animals)
  Includes bibliographical references and index.
  ISBN 978-1-4296-6064-8 (library binding)
  ISBN 978-1-4296-7095-1 (paperback)
  1. Sea otter—Infancy—Juvenile literature. I. Title. II. Series.
  QL737.C25R87 2012
  599.769'5139—dc22
                                    2010053926

Summary: Full-color photographs and simple text describe how sea otter pups grow up.

Editorial Credits
Erika L. Shores, editor; Ashlee Suker, designer; Svetlana Zhurkin, media researcher; Laura Manthe, production specialist

Photo Credits
Ardea/Tom and Pat Leeson, 15
Dreamstime/Tommiddleton, 1, 21
iStockphoto/GomezDavid, 12–13
Minden Pictures/Doc White, 8–9; Sebastian Kennerknecht, cover; Suzi Eszterhas, 2–3, 4–5, 7
Photolibrary/Roberta Olenick, 11
SeaPics/Jane Vargas, 16–17, 19

Capstone Press thanks Suzann G. Speckman, PhD, with the Marine Mammals Management department
of the U.S. Fish and Wildlife Service, for her assistance in reviewing this book.

The author dedicates this book to her son Markus Johan Rustad.

Note to Parents and Teachers

The Baby Animals series supports national science standards related to life science.
This book describes and illustrates sea otter pups. The images support early readers in
understanding the text. The repetition of words and phrases helps early readers learn
new words. This book also introduces early readers to subject-specific vocabulary words,
which are defined in the Glossary section. Early readers may need assistance to read
some words and to use the Table of Contents, Glossary, Read More, Internet Sites, and
Index sections of the book.

Printed in the United States of America in North Mankato, Minnesota.
032011   006110CGF11

Index

Word Count: 201
Grade: 1
Early-Intervention Level: 18